GUIDE

INTRODUCTION

Pokémon Scarlet & Violet, the most recent Pokémon adventures for the Nintendo Switch, will debut on November 18, 2022.The first Pokémon games of this generation are those from Generation 9, which started with Pokémon Sword & Shield. The Paldea region is where the games are held. The following mainline games in the series, Pokémon Scarlet & Violet, continue the tradition that Pokémon Red & Blue established in the past and carried on through all successive generations, including Pokémon Sword & Shield. All the essential elements you'd identify with the primary Pokémon series are present in Scarlet & Violet: There is a wide world to discover, many people to get to know, and a plethora of Pokémon to catch and battle (some old, some new, friendly or hostile).

Prologue - First Day of School

First Day of School, the prologue of Pokemon Scarlet and Violet, functions as a guide for the game. You have a lot to do right away, like choosing your starter Pokémon, having your first trainer quarrel, and discovering how to catch wild Pokemon. Throughout this assignment, you will visit Cabo Poco, Poco Trail, Inlet Groto, the Lighthouse, Las Platos, and ultimately Mesagoza. In order to help you complete the quest, we'll guide you through each of the main storyline objectives in this walkthrough. Along with that, we've included details on goods you could find while exploring and optional trainer fights we think you should participate in for rewards.

Getting Started

Before the game begins, you may play about in a character creation menu and create your character there. By changing your hair, eye, and other traits, you can change how you seem. When you're happy with your design, start the game! Once your school application has been created, an introduction sequence will start playing. You will take control of your character while they sit at their home computer. An introductory tutorial will show you how to move about the game world and expose you to some basic gameplay concepts and story themes. When you come back downstairs, he'll ask you to meet him outside so you can choose your first Pokémon. The following three new Scarlet and Violet starting Pokémon are now available:

- Sprigatito - The Grass Cat Pokemon
- Quaxly - The Water-type Duckling Pokemon
- Fuecoco - The Fire Croc Pokemon

Before leaving for Cabo Poco, you'll have some alone time with them so you won't have to make a decision straight away. When you are ready to go, your mother will give you a Rotom phone. Using this, you can save programs like the Map App, which you may open at any time by pressing Y. Perform this action to reveal your next objective as soon as you regain control of your character.

The First Day of School

Now that the starter Pokemon is following you and your Rotom Phone is safely tucked away in your pocket, it's time to approach the first area of Cabo Poco.

A Visit to the Neighbor's - Cabo Poco

As part of the orders for this task, take the Pokemon you were given for a stroll before meeting Director Clavell at the adjacent house. But enter the vegetable garden on the south side of your house's right side before you leave. Here, you may buy an antidote. By turning around the house's back to the north, you can find a potion. After that, continue along the trail and turn left to reach a Poke Ball. Now is the time to descend to the Cabo Poco residence. Two characters that you encounter throughout the way can be spoken to. The woman on the right will greet you and provide information about Cabo Poco, while the man on the left will briefly explain the game's multiplayer features.

Before you reach the house, walk to the left and get the Poke Ball tucked away behind the tree. When you have this, enter the home via the gates, and Director Clavell and Nemona will greet you.You'll be given a tour of the school by Nemona, a different student at Naranja/Uva Academy, who will also provide you additional details on how to improve your combat skills as the game progresses. She'll also want to fight you anytime she gets the chance, so be prepared. But first, pick your starting point now!

Choosing Your Starter

There are three beginning Pokémon, as was already explained. You can interact with the Pokémon you're considering to learn more about their abilities.

- Sprigatito - The Grass Cat Pokemon is strong against **Water**
- Quaxly - The Water-type Duckling Pokemon is strong against **Fire**
- Fuecoco - The Fire Croc Pokemon is strong against **Grass**

Once you've made your choice, Nemona will want to challenge you, so she chose another Pokemon to raise alongside yours. She will select the entry-level variety that is weaker in comparison to yours. She will choose Quaxly if you choose Sprigatito, for instance. Whoever is still alive will be looked after by Director Clavell.Once she has chosen her starting point, Nemona will challenge you to a fight on the sand, and she swears to be there when you get there.

A Challenge from Nemona - Private Beach

- **Have your first Pokemon battle with Nemona on the beach.**

Before going to the beach, you need explore and get a few more items. Turn left and proceed east around the back of

the academy to the palm tree. Collect the Potion to learn more about Auto Heal. If you proceed south from here, you will see two things. One is a Potion off in the distance, while the other is an Antidote to the right. As you approach the shore, make your way to the left, but don't confront Nemona just yet. Turn south after reaching the water's edge. Right here, you can get the Poke Ball.
Face northeast and aim for Nemona. However, pass her and reach the narrow path that leads to the west's dead end. Go all the way to the end to obtain a Poke Ball.Get ready for your first battle, then return to the Nemona.

Pokemon Trainer Battle vs. Nemona
Use a move specific to your kind in your first Pokemon battle. For Sprigatito, we used Leafage to oppose Nemona's Quaxley. The move you use should be quite successful because Nemona's starter is entirely ineffectual compared to your starter's kind. Once the fighting is over, Nemona is eager to fight. But Clavell

will intervene and say that's plenty for today.

After this talk, you'll receive the Pokedex App for your Rotom Phone. You should now begin learning how to catch wild Pokémon and fill it up!

Nemona Leads the Way - Cabo Poco

- Let Nemona lead the way as she demonstrates how to catch wild Pokémon.

As you make your way back to the school gates from the west, you will encounter your mother and Nemona. In this area, Mom will offer you the Sandwich and 5 Potions. You can now enter the Poco Trail, which is your first Pokémon-containing locale.

Poco Path

Nemona will go with you to Poco Trail and show you how to catch the first wild Pokemon in the game. 5 Poke Balls will be given to you by her so you may try your luck at catching a few fresh Pokémon. Your initial objective will be a LeChonk.Press X and A to throw your

Poke Ball and try to catch it. When you speak with Nemona again, she'll give you 10 Poke Balls and let you explore at your leisure. She will give you instructions to meet her at the Lighthouse when you are ready.

To the Lighthouse

- Make your way to the massive lighthouse by traveling down Poco Trail.

The tree right in front of you (to the east of the map) should have a Poke Ball close by. Turn around and walk northwest to get the item—a Potion—from behind the rock. As you go farther east, you'll see some shining faraway objects and Pokemon ambling through the grass and along the road. If you continue up the road acquiring the Items that you can see out in the distance, the first one will be a Potion, the second one will be a Poke Ball, and the third one - in the very northern portion behind the tree - will be a Super Potion.

After obtaining the Revive, proceed to the south and locate the Antidote next to the barrier. Then go southeast. Southward journey is continued; climb the bluff. Look in the nook to the east to find the Rare Candy. Gather the Potion by traveling to the east. Continue farther east along the rope once you have the Paralyze Heal until you reach the top of the cliff. Near the two palm palms there, you may pick up the Revive. Turn around and continue along the ropes towards the west, then take the Revive and continue along the path northward. On your way up the path, Nemona will stop you. The conversation will abruptly come to a stop, and you'll go to look into a weird cry.

The Mysterious Cry

- Track down the origin of the weird shriek that erupted nearby!

Before you hurry off to check the sounds, there are a few things you should hang onto. Gather the ether next to the rock and then turn to the north. then do a U-turn and get the potion from the tree's

side. Continue on and drink another
potion when you reach the bigger tree in
the northwest. As you can see, there
ought to be something right behind this
one. Then proceed to return to the
eastward-pointing road after purchasing
an ether there. Near the trail's edge, look
for Nemona, then look behind her for the
broken wall. The next time you travel this
way, the howl will stop you in your tracks.
If you glance down, you may see a
mysterious Pokemon sleeping by the
water, surrounded by Houndour. You'll
stumble and land close to the Pokemon
on the sand. Get close to it and interact
with it. It is too feeble to move, so give it
the lunch your mother cooked. As a
consequence, it will be able to restore
some energy. It will suddenly get up and
advance toward the cave behind you.

Inlet Grotto

Grab the Potion in front of you as you
follow the Pokemon inside the cave. If
you keep going after the Pokemon, you'll
smash the rock. When you enter the

room to the left and in front of you, two extra objects are visible. The pokeball is on the left; take it. Take the Potion from the area next to the boulder, then proceed to the cave's back entrance to obtain the Revive. As you progress, following the Pokemon into the cave, Nemona will make an effort to help you. As you descend farther, a Houndoom will approach from behind. Your Pokemon will be entirely killed in the fight because this foe is a level 4 opponent. Luckily, the mysterious Pokémon will save you and show you how to leave the cave. You'll arrive directly in front of the Lighthouse outdoors. You'll get a call from Nemona and a TM032 Swift.

At the Lighthouse

Koraidon/Miraidon is the mysterious Pokemon you found, according to Arven, who you'll run into if you continue up the path to the Lighthouse. If you defeat him in a fight, you'll receive a Poke Ball for Koraidon or Miraidon.

Trainer Battle Against Pokemon Trainer Arven

Skwovet is most vulnerable to attacks of the Fighting sort. But because your Pokemon are surely at least Level 7 at this time, you should still be able to do some respectable damage as long as you aren't using Ghost-type attacks!

Atop the Lighthouse

- Go to the top of the Lighthouse by following Nemona.

Before climbing the lighthouse, get a Revive from behind it. Take in the view of Mesagoza and the structure containing the Poke Ball while conversing with Nemona while perched atop the Lighthouse.

Los Platos

- Get yourself over to Los Platos!

On the drive to Los Platos, you can see a Pokemon Center off in the distance. As you proceed in that manner, you will come across young Elian, who you may battle along the way, on the left just before the bridge. To combat Elian, we advise bringing in a Flying-type Pokémon. You should be able to get in touch with one who is nearby. Use Fuecoco, though, if it was your starter, immediately away. Once Elian has been vanquished, head northeast to get the X Defense. Take a trip to Los Platos in the northwest to join the Awakening. While traveling west after turning around will get you the Potion, it will get you the Poke Ball next to the water. The Poke Ball is in the southwest; find another one by going south. Just before you cross the bridge into Los Platos, there is one final fight you can have with Zahira the Student. Find Nemona first near Los Platos' entrance, close to the Pokemon Center. She will provide you materials and League Points that you can utilize at the Pokemon Center to build TMs.

The City of Mesagoza

- Arrive in Mesagoza, where a new school is waiting for you.

The objectives will change to persuade you to move on to Mesagoza even though there is a lot to gather and trainers to confront in Los Platos. Travel west and then southwest to find the Antidote. At the back of the gardens, locate a Paralyze Heal. Take the RestTM at this point and move westward toward the body of water. Exit Los Platos via the west exit, then turn northwest just after the exit to get a potion and an exp. candy XS. Additionally, at the extreme northwest corner, there is a Stored Power TM. As you would ordinarily, leave Los Platos, then turn left to reach the Antidote on the west side. Up the slope you go until you come to the Poke Ball. Then, head south and ascend closer to the cliff to get the net ball. Battle Pere the Student as you get back to the highway. Once Pere has been vanquished, turn to the northeast and approach this Potion. To confront Ruben the Janitor, continue north along the path to the right after obtaining the Poke Ball from the boulder in the northwest. After obtaining the Poke Ball, move east to locate the X Sp.

Def close to the settlement. Making sure to snag the Potion and Antidote nearby, turn around and head back to the trail in a westerly direction. For the Poke Ball and Exp. Candy XS, keep traveling north over the grass in the direction of the walkway. The Pokémon Center and a different trainer should now be visible. Instead of going on to Mesagoza, we suggest turning around and going back to Los Platos to gather more supplies and fight a couple more battles. Your first find in the direction of the east should be an ether.Youngster Luka, another trainer you must battle, will appear as you proceed farther down the path.As you continue on your journey toward Los Platos, you may discover two more items in the grass to the northwest. Grab the Burn Heal and Poke Ball, then head southwest to find a Paralyze Heal.Return to the path and interact with Carlota the Student, a different instructor.A second potion and an antidote can be found adjacent to Los Platos and beneath the rock to her south.

Cut the grass over before you enter Mesagoza from the north. Look through the grass for any items you may have missed, like a potion close to a boulder just to the north of Los Platos.When you return to the area near Mesagoza's entrance, proceed to the Pokemon Center. Here, speak with the Pokemon League representative. He will reward you with a Thunder Wave TM if you have been following our guidance after you meet his demand to vanquish 4 trainers in combat in the South Province (Area One).

Stony Cliff Titan

How to Prepare for Klawf, the Stony Cliff Titan

We've included a table showing the recommended level you should be at before starting this quest, the Pokemon you should have on your team, and the potential rewards.

How to Find Klawf, the Stony Cliff Titan

After leaving Mesagoza, enter South Province through the east gate (Area Three). Approach Pikachu who is sitting at the picnic table on the left. You can make use of these picnic tables whenever your Pokemon needs to unwind. By speaking to the man at the table, you might get a variety of items to utilize in building your own sandwiches.collect the Potion next to the boulder after heading east, then go up and to the left to collect the Poke Doll. While you're here, you can choose to battle the student who is currently pursuing the rock.

Trainer Name	Pokemon (w/ LV.)	Type
Martina the Student	Arrokuda (LV. 11)	Water

You can pick up the Potion on the right while you're here. Follow the trail north, up and around, and stay on it. Once you see the sign that reads "To Artazon, The Village of Nature and Art," turn southeast into the grass and around the back of the mountain. Here, something called a revive needs to be gathered. Return to the sign (just past the sign) after obtaining the Super Potion close to the tree on the right.

The summit of the northbound trail is where Sam the Backpacker is located. Before approaching him in battle, slide down the southwest-facing route to the left and acquire the Great Ball. Before fighting Backpacker Samuel, climb back up and grab the Zinc from behind.

Trainer Name	Pokemon (w/ LV.)	Type
Backpacker Samuel	Starly (LV. 11)	Normal/Flying

Continuing north will bring you to the Energy Root. Then proceed north to get the Antidote and X Speed. Continue on your quest until you see Alicia the Musician at the Pokémon Center.

Trainer Name	Pokemon (w/ LV.)	Type
Alicia the Musician	Igglybuff (LV. 11)	Normal/Fairy

Additionally, right behind Alicia to the northwest is a Parazlye Heal.You should head to the Pokémon Center if you need to unwind. If not, you can speak to the Pokemon League Representative nearby, who will let you know that you must defeat 6 trainers in this region in order to receive a prize. As you move to the northwest, engage Severino the Office Worker in combat.

Trainer Name	Pokemon (w/ LV.)	Type
Severino the Office Worker	Jigglypuff (LV. 17) / Skiddo (LV. 17)	Normal/Fairy and Grass

Follow the path to Artazon. Take advantage of the Hasty Mint that can be present after you enter the new area. There is a chance that Benjamin the Student and I will get into another argument.

Trainer Name	Pokemon (w/ LV.)	Type
Benjamin the Student	Sunkern (LV. 12) / Bonsly (LV. 12)	Grass / Rock

As you approach the cliff's edge in the northeast, pick up the Full Heal. Take the Rare Candy from the cliff's edge heading west as you travel northeast. Returning to the northeast, visit the tower to obtain the Awakening. Talk to the person on the picnic bench to get extra ingredients and take a rest if necessary.

Before choosing the path down, head to the left-hand track that climbs to the rock. Make your way south after getting the Potion. the Southeast Exp. Candy XS. collect it. After that, go northeast to where you may pick up the lemonade. Turn around and take the Exp. Candy XS off the rock. Grab the Ultra Ball from the grass facing east, then make your way north to the rocks to get the X Defense. If you keep walking north, you will soon observe the Stony Cliff Titan climbing the rocky wall. Continue down the path that ascends to the right until the cutscene begins.

How to Beat Klawf, the Stony Cliff Titan

If you started with a Grass or Water Pokemon, Klawf should be simple to beat since it is a Rock-type Pokemon. If you select Fuecoco, you can attack here with a Pokemon of the Grass, Water, or Ground types. Once you've hit Klawf a few times, it will move and plummet to the route below.When you continue after it has lost some health, the Titan Klawf will open the cave, allowing you to enter. It will consume the herb in the cave to develop strength. Thankfully, Arven will support you in this battle against Klawf. Just use the same Pokemon and repeat your plan from the first battle.

Stony Cliff Titan Rewards

Arven and you should enter the cave after you've defeated Klawf. Purchase Sweet Herba Mystica and deliver your sandwich to Koraidon/Miraidon here. After Koraidon/Miraidon defeats the Stony Cliff Titan and consumes the Sweet Herba Mystica, Pokemon may Dash. Moving across the map will go much more quickly now that you are aware of this, which is why we advised doing it first. We won't be going back to Artazon until the sixth trainer has to be defeated in order to unlock the prize from the Pokemon Center for South Province (Area Three), even though you will already have fought five of the six trainers needed to get it. For now, return to Mesagoza, then turn west to confront the Cortondo Gym (Bug).

Cortondo Gym (Bug)

How to Prepare for Cortondo Gym (Bug)

Before using this Bug-type Gym, you must have battled the Titan from the Stony Cliff in order to learn a new travel ability. This will give you the chance to train more and level up your Pokemon till they reach the recommended level for success in this gym.To avoid early spoilers, we've hidden the reward you'll get for completing this Bug Gym, but if you're curious, click to find out more!

How to Find the Cortondo Gym (Bug)

Turning west from Mesagoza will get you to South Province (Area Two). You should follow this path as it leads to Cortondo in the east. As you embark on your trip to gather various items, you can speak with the woman sitting at the picnic table. A little higher up from her, you ought to be able to see a girl hidden beneath a tree.

Alongside her, there is also a Poke Doll. If you want to start a fight after getting this, go talk to the female. You must eliminate 5 Trainers in South Province (Area 2) in order to obtain a Prize.

Trainer Name	Pokemon (w/ LV.)	Type
Noa the Student	Scatterbug (LV. 8) / Drifloon (LV. 8)	Bug and Ghost / Flying

Continue along the road to the left and you will find a Paralyze Heal and Poke Ball. You can battle Sergio the Office Worker, a man dressed professionally, who is there a few ways up.

Trainer Name	Pokemon (w/ LV.)	Type
Sergio the Office Worker	Wooper (LV. 8)	Poison / Ground

only stopping to grab the ether laying in the grass to the west and the ether lying on the cliff edge to the northeast as they traveled along the route. Visit the Pokemon Center to obtain the potion in the north.Return to the route close to the Pokemon Center after picking up the Paralyze Heal in the west. After descending to the base of the cliff, turn southeast and collect the Poke Ball by the tree and the Super Potion close to the crystals. Turn around and return to the north to get the Paralyze Heal and the Potion by the tree.

Trainer Name	Pokemon (w/ LV.)	Type
Alba the Waitress	Pichu (LV. 9)	Electric

When you arrive back on the path, you can also encounter awakenings in the field just to the route's left. Before entering the Pokemon Center, make your way over to the office worker who is standing at the T-intersection of the path..

Trainer Name	Pokemon (w/ LV.)	Type
David the Office Worker	Phanpy (LV. 9)	Ground

After this battle, turn around and proceed to Cortondo. You can face another adversary on this road if you turn southeast.

Trainer Name	Pokemon (w/ LV.)	Type
Angel the Courier	Psyduck (LV. 14) / Maschiff (LV. 14) / Mudbray (LV. 14)	Water and Dark and Ground

In the direction of Cortondo, get back to the Pokemon Center. Take a break if you need to, but make sure to talk to the Pokemon League representative that is present. You must defeat 5 Trainers in the South Province (Area Two) at his request. As you enter Cortondo, the Gym lies to your immediate south. When you arrive, Nemona will be there. She will give you a few things and tell you that before you confront the gym leader at each gym, you must pass the gym test. Speak to the person at the counter to reserve this one, the Olive Roll.

How to Pass the Gym Test - Olive Roll

For this test, a sizable Olive is placed in an obstacle course with you. The goal is to roll the olive-shaped ball all the way to the end and put it in the goal basket. To find the olive field (which is the basket), head to the town's north side and look for the big square. Once the test has begun, push the Olive through the maze. Simply give it a gentle tap to move it, then navigate the bends while avoiding the ramps and pedestrians. Once you push it into the basket at the finish line and return to the gym, you can challenge Gym Leader Katy.

Challenge the Cortondo Gym Leader Katy

Lv.	Pokemon
Lv. 14	Nymble
Lv. 14	Tarantoula
Lv. 15	Teddiursa

Here, fire-type Pokemon displayed excellent performance by dispatching all of Katy's Pokemon in a single move. You can also use attacks of the Flying and Rock categories to achieve victory.

Cortondo Gym Rewards

After defeating Gym Leader Katy, you are given TM021 Pounce and have a simpler time gathering Lv. 25 Pokemon. Additionally, they'll pay attention to you, which will make them easier to control in battle. After defeating this gym, fly as close as you can to Artazon, preferably to the Pokemon Center in South Province (Area Three), which is located immediately after Mesagoza. Our next stop is the Artazon Gym (Grass)!

Artazon Gym (Grass)

How to Prepare for Artazon Gym (Grass)

Before taking on this Grass-type Gym, you ought to be level 17 and have a team of Pokemon that can handle the challenge. When fighting a gym that uses Grass-type Pokemon, we'd suggest using Fire-type moves in addition to Flying and Bug-type attacks. There are further types of Pokemon that grass-type Pokemon are susceptible to, but you've probably already come across some of these in the starting areas (or at least ones that can use those exact attacks). To avoid early spoilers, we've hidden the reward you'll get for completing this Bug Gym, but if you're curious, click to find out more!

Recommend Level	Recommended Pokemon	Rewards Upon Completion
17	Fire, Flying, and Bug-type	TM020 Trailblaze

How to Find the Artazon Gym (Grass)

If you fly back to the Pokemon Center that is closest to where you defeated Klawf, you'll be near Artazon. You should find the Burn Heal close to the sign and the Awakening here when you travel east into Artazon proper. On the north side of the rock wall, before entering Artazon, you can face Cristina the Student and get a Great Ball.

Trainer Name	Pokemon (w/ LV.)	Type
Cristina the Student	Gastly (LV. 13) / Murkrow (LV. 13)	Ghost / Poison and Dark / Flying

After this conflict, proceed to take the Burn Heal from the grass. The path will now split, with Artazon on the right and Amaia the Student, another trainer you can encounter, on the left.

Trainer Name	Pokemon (w/ LV.)	Type
Amaia the Student	Happiny (LV. 13) / Drifloon (LV. 8)	Normal and Ghost / Flying

The Exp. Candy XS can be found by turning left at this point and heading northwest while descending the slope. Turn south and ascend the rock once you have the Max Ether. Next, turn northeast to locate three items to collect on this raised area. A Poke Doll on the right, a Hyper Potion on the left, and the Guard Spec will be the ones nearest to you. Take some fresh water from the top of the rock to the south before proceeding to enter Artazon. As you enter Artazon, the gym is on the southern side. As you enter, Nemona will approach you and hand you numerous things. To find out more about the exact Gym Exam you must pass in order to confront Brassius, go over to the desk. The Sunflora Lawn, which is immediately to the right of the gym as you leave, is where you can find out more about it. The game is called Sunflora Hide-and-Seek.

How to Pass the Gym Test - Sunflora Hide-and-Seek

You must collect and deliver 10 Sunflora, as revealed by speaking with the woman outside the Sunflora Lawn. All across Artazon, you can find Sunflora, and they will stick with you as you acquire new ones. Turn around as soon as the work begins; some of them should be in your rear. You will then only need to look about the town for the remaining ones. They are widely dispersed in Artazon and are easily found if you just explore as much of the area as you can. One will run away if you try to approach it, and you'll have to fight it off to get it. Use the specified Pokémon types to quickly beat the Sunflora here. You can challenge the gym leader once you have all 10 by going back to the gym.

Challenge the Artazon Gym Leader Brassius

Lv.	Pokemon
Lv. 16	Petilil
Lv. 16	Smoliv
Lv. 17	Sudowoodo

In this battle, you can also use attacks of the Fire, Flying, or Insect categories. Sudowoodoo is the one who terastallizes and gains strength. If a Pokemon of the Fire type is used here, its attacks will be Extremely Effective. We used a Litleo and Ember Attack to get rid of Sudowoodo.

Artazon Gym Rewards

After fighting Brassius, you'll get two gym badges, which make it easier to catch Pokemon up to level 30. They'll also conduct lot more responsibly and follow your instructions. You will also receive TM020 Trailblaze.After the fight is over, return to the gym's entrance where you'll find Hassel, one of the Pokemon League's Elite Four.

Open Sky Titan
How to Prepare for Bombirdier, the Open Sky Titan

Recommend Level	Recommended Pokemon	Rewards Upon Completion
19	Rock, Fairy and Electric-type	Swim for Mount

How to Find Bombirdier, the Open Sky Titan

Take the route into West Province (Area One) after leaving Cortondo and turning west. When you're done, you should see the first trainer you saw along the route (who will be standing on the right) and a resource on the left (3 x Potion).

Trainer Name	Pokemon (w/ LV.)	Type
Yeray the Student	Fletchling (LV. 14)	Normal / Flying

As you ascend, stay on the trail and head north until you reach the curve, when you'll turn south. Here, you can fight alongside a different trainer.

Trainer Name	Pokemon (w/ LV.)	Type
Aroa the Student	Shuppet (LV. 14)	Ghost

Just a short ways up the trail on the left, you might find a Great Ball. If you continue down the winding road, the item should be glowing off by the rock near the lake, to the west, just before the third trainer. Get the Antidote there by going there. If you continue to move in the direction of the Open Sky Titan sign, you can find the third trainer just a short distance up past the Antidote.

Trainer Name	Pokemon (w/ LV.)	Type
Neizan the Student	Venonat (LV. 14)	Bug / Poison

As you proceed northwest on the walkway, look for a picnic table on the right. Before continuing, request a list of ingredients from the person at the pinic table. You could locate an X Speed on your right after the picnic table. There are even more items to discover as you advance! If you continue on the path, you'll shortly start traveling west and reach a bridge. A fourth trainer is located right over this bridge, near to the path's curve.

Trainer Name	Pokemon (w/ LV.)	Type
Backpacker Asier	Foongus (LV. 14)	Grass / Poison

After the fourth trainer, turn off the trail and start cutting through the grass toward the Pokemon Center. At this point, get the Rare Bone. If a break is necessary, go ahead and take it before resuming your hike.

Trainer Name	Pokemon (w/ LV.)	Type
Mireia the Musician	Meowth (LV. 15)	Normal

After the sixth trainer, on the right, is a Super Potion. As you head north, your phone will now begin to ring. When you approach the Open Sky Titan, Arven will utilize this to let you know. You'll come to a road fork with a picnic table in the middle.

Speak to the person at the picnic table to get a variety of ingredients. While you're here, you might as well engage in combat with the other trainer, who is to the right.

Trainer Name	Pokemon (w/ LV.)	Type
Enrique the Student	Pineco (LV. 15) / Nymble (LV. 15)	Bug and Bug

Before heading to the Open Sky Titan, don't forget to take a break at the picnic table.

How to Beat Bombirdier, the Open Sky Titan

You should turn left (westward) at the picnic table. While climbing the mountain's trail, you must watch out for falling rocks. Upon your arrival, a cutscene starring the stork-like Bombirdier will begin.In this circumstance, moves of the Rock, Fairy, and Electric types will all be effective. We used a Rockruff, and found that the Rock Throw attack rapidly eliminated Bombirdier. When you defeat it, it will follow Klawf's example and destroy the surrounding cave in order to obtain some Herba Mystica and refresh itself in order to become stronger.Arven will assist you in the second encounter with his Lv. 19 Nacli. This will employ techniques like Smack Down, which will likewise be quite successful. Use the suggested kinds and attacks as you did in the first round of this battle. Nonetheless, be careful since Bombardier can utilize Torment to prohibit you from using the same move twice in a row.

Open Sky Titan Rewards

Arven will go with you back into the cave if you are successful the second time and manage to find the Bitter Herba Mystica. You can now ride the mysterious Pokémon across the sea since you gave it to Koraidon/Miriadan.You'll understand why Arven is so committed to finding these giants and the Herba Mystica once you've finished this one. You'll receive a call as you leave advising you to keep an eye on Koraidon/Miriadan and informing you once more about Aero Zero.

Team Star Dark Crew - Giacomo
How to Prepare for Team Star Dark Crew

Recommend Level	Recommended Pokemon	Rewards Upon Completion
21	Electric, Rock, Bug, and Fighting-type	TM062 Foul Play

How to Find Team Star Dark Crew Base

You'll be moving from West Province to Team Star's Dark Crew HQ (Area One) if you've been following our advice. If you took a different path, you should head in this direction. We advise completing the Open Flying Titan mission before beginning this assignment; following that, go toward the northeast. From the picnic table adjacent to the bridge, turn northeast to find the route leading to West Province (Area One - North). After going over the bridge from the picnic table, take the first trail on the right. Here, Candina the Model is your opponent.

Trainer Name	Pokemon (w/ LV.)	Type
Candina the Model	Oinkologne (LV. 20) / Luxio (LV. 20)	Normal and Electric

Until it connects with the one on the bottom left, continue northeast along this route. You'll have to fight against another trainer here.

Trainer Name	Pokemon (w/ LV.)	Type
Backpacker Mateo	Eevee (LV. 15)	Normal

In order to receive your prize from the Pokemon League Rep along the road, head northeast in the direction of the Pokémon Center until you approach the last Pokemon Trainer.

Trainer Name	Pokemon (w/ LV.)	Type
Yasmin the Student	Teddiursa (LV. 16) / Tinkatink (LV. 16)	Normal and Fairy/Steel

Go to the Pokémon Center, take a break if necessary, and speak with the Pokemon League Rep there. Just in front of the flags indicating the location of Giacomo's

The Pokemon Center is where Team Star Dark Crew's headquarters are. By now, you need to have faced nine Pokemon Trainers. Speak with the representative to obtain a Clear Amulet.Take three Great Balls as you approach the gate as you continue to move toward the base. Since you won't be able to combat the grunts close to the blocked road, you must proceed up and to the right to find Giacomo and his company. Before you enter, grab the X Sp. Def, and then proceed to Team Star's Dark Crew headquarters. By conversing with the grunts, you might discover that Giacomo is the leader of Team Star's Dark Crew, commonly known as the Segin Squad. To get entrance, you must take down Team Star Grunt A, the base's guard.

Lv.	Pokemon	Type
Lv. 19	Murkrow	Dark/Flying

We advise employing Pokemon with Electric and Rock-type moves for this match. Here, Pawmi and Rockruff were utilized, and it worked really well.Team Star Grunt B will enter the base and inform the other members that you have arrived. You'll receive a call from Cassiopeia informing you that you must battle waves of Pokemon in a battle known as a Star Barrage in order to vanquish them. But only the first three Pokemon in your party may be used, therefore you should arrange them here. The Dark Pokemon in Team Star will be weak to those, so switch to these Pokemon kinds before continuing. Fighting and Bug-type Pokemon are your best chance here.

How Star Barrage Works

You have ten minutes to annihilate as many as thirty Pokemon during a Star Barrage. Choose three Pokemon of the Fighting and Bug types for this one because the Star Crew will be vulnerable to those types. To send your three Pokemon out and begin the battle at the same time as the timer, press R.

In particular, we advise doing this frequently if you lose any Pokemon. To help them recover, Clive will be there. Utilize any of the scattered vending machines to refill your Pokemon. If you fail all three, the challenge must be restarted. When this happens, you'll also receive advice on the Pokemon varieties you should be using.Giacomo will, however, appear if you beat 30 in the allocated time.

Lv.	Pokemon
Lv. 21	Pawniard
Lv. 20	Revaroom - Segin Starmobile

Pokemon with Fighting and Bug-type attacks should be used to fight Giacomo.

Rewards for Beating Giacomo

You'll watch a flashback involving each member of Team Star once you defeat Giacomo. Giacomo hands you TM062 Foul Play in addition to his Star Badge. After the battle, Cassiopeia will call and give you 5,000 LP plus some resources so you may make the new TMs that the base's completion will unlock.

Levincia Gym (Electric)

How to Prepare for Levincia Gym (Electric)

Electric-type Fortunately, Gym Leader Iono will utilize Pokemon that are not exclusively of the Electric type. Pokemon are renowned for being excellent defensively. This increases the variety of Pokemon you may select for your party, which is why we've included several different move types below.

Recommend Level	Recommended Pokemon	Rewards Upon Completion
24	Ground, Rock-type	TM048 Volt Switch

How to Find the Levincia Gym (Electric)

After defeating Giacomo, we advise returning to Artazon and leaving from the northeast of the settlement. You will reach East Province by doing this (Area One). The Pokemon Center may be reached by following the way northeast.

Salvador the Janitor should be on your left as you start down the route.

Trainer Name	Pokemon (w/ LV.)	Type
Salvador the Janitor	Mareanie (LV. 17)	Poison / Water

Collect the ether right off the route, to the northwest, and behind the tree as you continue on the path. Go back to the walkway and move in the direction of the Pokémon Center. Eleonor the Chef is seen on the right.

Trainer Name	Pokemon (w/ LV.)	Type
Eleonor the Cook	Slowpoke (LV. 17)	Water / Psychic

Take a break in the Center if necessary, then talk to the Pokemon League Rep for the East Province (Area One). You must defeat 5 trainers, he will inform you. You will currently have 2/5, therefore we will work on collecting the remaining portion later.

The Super Potion may be found on the cliff wall on the right after turning around to the west on the route. The Big Ball may be found right on the water's edge if you turn around and go along this wall to the north. Return to the Pokémon Center at this time. Go north, over the hill, and then in the direction of the water's edge. This is where you want to go; keep going east. By the water, pick up the Great Ball, then head east. You can grab an ether from the right just before you reach the trainer on the left. Keep moving forward and grab the Super Potion before going to the trainer.

Now confront Xavier the Student by moving over to the water.

Trainer Name	Pokemon (w/ LV.)	Type
Xavier the Student	Kirlia (LV. 23) / Zangoose (LV. 23) / Noibat (LV. 23)	Psychic / Fairy and Normal and Flying / Dragon

Following this battle, dive in and proceed east once you can move around on water. You may trek up the slope to enter East Province after emerging from the sea (Area Two).Turn left and go up to the child here to fight as soon as you get to the grass.

Trainer Name	Pokemon (w/ LV.)	Type
Lina the Student	Cubchoo (LV. 21)	Ice

To join the trail, you need now move toward the north. Going west and down the trail will allow you to pick up a few additional battles en route rather than heading straight into Levincia.If you do, Backpacker Arturo will be the first person you see on the right.

Trainer Name	Pokemon (w/ LV.)	Type
Backpacker Arturo	Sandile (LV. 21)	Ground / Dark

Walk the trail to the southwest. You may see something on the right as you approach the bend where you'll start heading north. Go northwest after obtaining the Super Potion until you encounter the following Pokemon Trainer.

Trainer Name	Pokemon (w/ LV.)	Type
Beatriz the Student	Alomomola (LV. 20)	Water

Make your way to the Pokemon Center in the west, immediately before the bridge, after this battle. Once you clear the way, you will be able to quickly move through it thanks to this. You may find a Psychic Terrain TM by the tree beside the Pokémon Center on the left. Go northeast, current over the lake, and towards the ruins here, with the Levincia Gym as your destination. To locate another foe to fight, head behind the ruins (and to the north) after stopping by the ruins to pick up the Toxic Spike TM.

Trainer Name	Pokemon (w/ LV.)	Type
Ramon the Student	Rufflet (LV. 23) / Drednaw (LV. 23)	Normal / Flying and Water / Rock

Now head east, then make a little bend to the northeast close to the tree to get the Magical LeafTM. Continue in this manner until you encounter the rock and the student hiding behind it.

Trainer Name	Pokemon (w/ LV.)	Type
Rosario the Student	Oricorio (LV. 24) / Houndoom (LV. 24)	Fire / Flying and Dark / Fire

We're going to cut over the grass and move in the direction of Levincia Gym, which will now be immediately to the east. Go south instead than right off the cliff as you approach the edge. If you wish to fight another trainer before entering the city, follow this down to the beginning of Levincia (on the right).

Trainer Name	Pokemon (w/ LV.)	Type
Cristian the Office Worker	Klefki (LV. 22)	Steel / Fairy

Speak with the Pokemon League Representative by coming over to the Pokémon Center. To receive a reward, you must defeat 6 Pokémon Trainers in East Province (Area 2). You should have this and will be given a Stomping Tantrum TM if you have been following this instructions.

Inside Levincia

In order to go to the second building on the right after entering, use the main walkway (the one to the left of the Pokemon Center). An Exp. Candy XS is a collectible that may be found here. Just before you reach the gym, keep walking down this route and take a right turn. Under the chair and umbrellas, there are two Paralyze Heals. Turn right just before the gym. Find the X Accuracy close to the planter by taking that way down there.Turn toward the north, cross the lawn, and then return to the front of the gym to acquire Wise Glasses. Before entering, proceed west to the flowerbed and palm tree next to the yellow below. You can get a hold of the Struggle Bug TM behind this.

Now make your way to the gym. As soon as you enter, Nemona will phone to arrange to meet you there. Whichever discussion option you select, she will demand that you take part in a pre-Gym combat. When you are on the fight court, she advises that you should try to find a practice court nearby before entering any gyms.

Pokémon Battle Against Nemona

Lv.	Pokémon
Lv. 21	Rockruff
Lv. 21	Pawmi
Lv. 22	Starter

We urged Pokemon to use Ground-type attacks at the beginning of this post, and that is exactly what you should do here against Nemona's Rockruff and Pawmi. She will then throw away her starter Pokémon and use her Tera Orb. You don't always need to use your Tera Orb if your starter Pokémon is at or near this level. However, if you do, save it for this round of combat.For beating Nemona, you are awarded 3 Full Heals. You'll be ready to hear more about the details of the current Gym Battle Test when you return to the gym's main desk. Iono is a streamer, so the test is to watch her stream.

How to Pass the Gym Test - Find Mr. Walksabout

Take a stroll outside, where Iono will explain the idea behind the gym exam and give you tips on how to succeed. You will be informed that you are being livestreamed and that your objective is to find... In several locations, director Clavell is playing hide and seek.You'll view security camera footage, and it's your job to spot Director Clavell in each tape. You must complete this challenge three times before you can face Iono. You'll have to fight a trainer each time you locate Clavell successfully.Here, we've included images of both Clavell's location for each round and the trainers and Pokemon you'll face off against.

- Locate Clavell in the sidewalk beside the seats.

Gym Trainer Marti will test you after you've located him.

Trainer Name	Pokemon (w/ LV.)
Gym Trainer Marti	Luxio (LV. 22)

- Visit the Pokémon Center to find Clavell.

After you've located him, Michael, the gym trainer, will test your mettle.

Trainer Name	Pokemon (w/ LV.)
Gym Trainer Michael	Tynamo (LV. 22) / Flaaffy (LV. 22)

- In the boat to the right of the combat court, locate Clavell.

After you locate him a third time, you'll get the chance to take on Iono. You will now be back at the desk at Levincia Gym and prepared to face Iono. Visit the Pokémon Center to give your Pokemon a rest if necessary.

Challenge the Levincia Gym Leader Iono

Lv.	Pokemon
Lv. 22	Wattrel
Lv. 23	Luxio
L. 23	Bellibolt
Lv. 23	Mismagius

Levincia Gym Rewards

Iono will reward you with the TM048 Volt Switch and declare that you can now easily handle Lv 35 Pokemon when you defeat her.The Pokemon League Chairperson, Geeta, will reappear in the gym lobby to let you know that your achievements haven't gone unnoticed.

Team Star Fire Crew - Mela

How to Prepare for Team Star Fire Crew

Recommend Level	Recommended Pokemon	Rewards Upon Completion
27	Water, Ground and Rock-type	TM038 Flame Charge

How to Find Team Star Fire Crew Base

You have two options for leaving the east gate: either fly back to Artazon or go to the Pokémon Center in East Province (Area One). You can't cross a barricade if you take this route after turning left at the Pokemon Center, and the base of the Team Star Fire Crew is immediately to your left.As you approach the base, you'll have to battle the Team Star Grunt A that is defending it.

Lv.	Pokemon	Type
Lv. 25	Houndour	Dark/Fire

How Star Barrage Works

You have ten minutes to annihilate as many as thirty Pokemon during a Star Barrage. For this one, water-type Pokemon are what you want because the goal is to choose 3 Pokemon that the Star Crew's Pokemon are weak against. To send your three Pokemon out and begin the battle at the same time as the timer, press R. In particular, we advise doing this frequently if you lose any Pokemon. To help them recover, Clive will be there. Utilize any of the scattered vending machines to refill your Pokemon. If you fail all three, the challenge must be restarted. If this occurs, you'll also learn which Pokemon varieties you should be using.However, Mela will appear if you defeat 30 in the allocated time.

Challenge Mela, Team Star's Fire Crew Boss

Lv.	Pokemon
Lv. 27	Torkoal
Lv. 26	Revaroom - Schedar Starmobile

Torkoal and the Schedar Starmobile are both weak to Rock, Water, and Ground-type attacks, so you have a few options here for the Pokemon you could add to your team.

Rewards for Beating Mela

A flashback involving each member of Team Star will appear after Mela is defeated, much like it did with Giacomo. You will also receive her Star Badge and TTM038 Flame Charge from her. Cassiopeia will get in touch with you when the battle is complete and give you 6,000 LP in addition to the materials you need to create the new TMs that will be made available once the base is finished.

How to Prepare for Orthworm, the Lurking Steel Titan

Recommend Level	Recommended Pokemon	Rewards Upon Completion
28	Fire, Fighting, or Ground-type Pokemon	High Jump for Mount

How to Find Orthworm, the Lurking Steel Titan

Exit Levincia Gym via the north road, then enter East Province (Area 2) and East Province (Area 3). Mark the Lurking Steel Titan as your destination when you start up the trail to make it simpler to stay on track. As you get closer to the top of the slope, start ascending to the northeast, where a trainer may be found on the right.

Trainer Name	Pokemon (w/ LV.)	Type
Ernesto the Student	2 x Oinkologne (LV. 23)	Normal

When you finally get to the top, a number of roads, challenges, and places to descend will become visible. You'll reach Orthworm the quickest by following the road that heads west.At the peak, the trail diverges into a cave to the left and to the right. Before following the left-hand road, you should first approach the other trainer in this region so that you can fight him.

Trainer Name	Pokemon (w/ LV.)	Type
Oliver the Worker	Varoom (LV. 23)	Steel/Poison

Follow the path to the left and pick up the Great Ball along the way. You will soon encounter Lea the Student, another trainer, if you continue in this direction.

Trainer Name	Pokemon (w/ LV.)	Type
Lea the Student	Snover (LV. 24)	Grass/Ice

Ascend the western mountain until you come to a right curve (next to the Lurking Steel Titan sign). Turn right to approach the cave's entrance, being cautious to collect the nearby Max Ether.As you approach, Orthworm will begin to race over the ground and attempt to flee from you.

Follow it and keep moving toward it until the exclamation point appears to signal the start of the combat.

How to Beat Orthworm, Lurking Steel Titan

Attacks of the Fire, Fighting, and Ground categories will be your best bet in this battle. Utilize these attacks frequently to reduce its health. Just prior to exiting the cave, Orthworm will drill a hole. In contrast to the previous Titan Pokemon that demolished the caverns and consumed Herba Mystica, Orthworm will run from this area. Pass through the tunnel and head east. You'll need to follow it as it travels underground once more for a while. Eventually, it will create another hole and eat some Herba Mystica to bolster its strength. The next battle is then necessary! As expected, Arven will appear and aid you in the subsequent battle. Arven will use a Toedscool at level 28. You should keep employing attacks of the Fire, Fighting, and Ground categories in this round. If

Toedscool uses supersonic to confuse the Lurking Steel Titan during combat and inflict damage on it, you should be able to significantly weaken it with Fire, Fighting, and Ground-type attacks.

Lurking Steel Titan Rewards

Once the fighting is over, you and Arven can go inside to find the Salty Herba Mystica. If you hold down the B button, you can split your sandwich and make bigger jumps.

Cascarrafa Gym (Water)

How to Prepare for Cascarrafa Gym (Water)

Recommend Level	Recommended Pokemon	Rewards Upon Completion
29	Grass-type	TM022 Chilling Water

How to Find the Cascarrafa Gym (Water)

You should head to the Pokémon Center in West Province (Area One) after defeating the Lurking Steel Titan. There will be a Team Star Dark Crew Base nearby. Giacomo has been defeated, thus you can proceed on the open road in the direction of Cascarrafa. You may see the Pokémon Center in front of you if you keep traveling along this northeastern path until you encounter a Pokemon Trainer on your right.

Trainer Name	Pokemon (w/ LV.)	Type
Alfredo the Student	Magikarp (LV. 16) / Arrokuda (LV. 16)	Water and Water

When you get to Cascarrafa, move to the south side. You must find the elevator that is positioned against the wall in order to access the Water Gym. Kofu, the gym's leader, will run out the door as soon as you approach, followed by the front desk employee. Kofu was reportedly racing to get something from Porto Marinada when he realized he had forgotten his wallet. If you want to pass the gym test, the receptionist at the gym will give you Kofu's wallet and urge you to give it back to him.

Head to Porto Marinada

From the north gate, leave Cascaraffa and head straight for the Asado Desert. After arriving in Porto Marinada, proceed across the Asado Desert to the west. You'll be able to tell when you're close by by seeing the Pokemon Center and Kofu because they're close to where the trail splits. After a cutscene, he will bolt off in the direction of Porto Marinada while shouting that he needs to go to the market.Go to the town's central square to find the market once you follow him inside.

In Porto Marinada

Kofu is in Porto Marinada, and the trainer will challenge you to a fight before he reports his wallet missing.

LV	Pokemon
LV. 28	Floatzel
LV. 28	Clauncher

Use grass-type Pokemon to do Hugo's team a ton of harm. Kofu will appear after the combat, and you can return his wallet to him.However, before you can engage Kofu in combat, you must help him get the rare relic he came for.

How to Pass the Gym Test - Win the Auction

For Cascaraffa, winning the auction entails passing the gym test. Bid modestly and just 5,000 at a time, and you'll find that passing is simple. The others will eventually give up and let you grab the ingredients.

Challenge the Cascaraffa Gym Leader Kofu

You'll need to return to Cascaraffa in order to face Kofu. Fly back here, then proceed to the south to use the elevator to ascend to the top floor and reach the gym.

Lv.	Pokemon
Lv. 29	Veluza
Lv. 29	Wugtrio
Lv. 30	Crabominable

Team Star Poison Crew – Atticus

How to Prepare for Team Star Poison Crew

Recommend Level	Recommended Pokemon	Rewards Upon Completion
32	Fire, Psychic and Ground-type	TM102 Gunk Shot

How to Find Team Star Poison Crew Base

From where you defeated the Lurking Steel Titan, proceed west along the East Province (Area Three) road. Grab the Revive on the left, just past the cave entrance you use to find the Lurking Steel Titan. This will take you to a Full Heal a short distance off to the left of the path if you follow it. As you continue, a portable Pokémon Center will be on your right. Near the corner, just next to the sign, you could discover a Hyper Potion. Next, you should look to the left to find the next two items. A Super Potion may be discovered initially next to the rocks, then an Elixir may be discovered high atop a hill directly to the west. From the larger mound on the left, Candy S., take this path until you reach the XP. The Super Potion can then be taken from the crater by heading north and descending from here. Return to the path and travel westward. You can engage in combat with a different trainer after obtaining the potion along this route.

Trainer Name	Pokemon (w/ LV.)	Type
Backpacker Lander	Impidimp (LV. 24)	Dark/Fairy

You can find a Timer Ball as you move along the path and come close to the bend that starts to take you off to the north. Stay on this trail after it makes a U-turn to the west. When you get there, fight the Pokemon Trainer who is right in front of the Pokémon Center.

Trainer Name	Pokemon (w/ LV.)	Type
Lorenzo the Student	Finneon (LV. 25) / Qwilfish (LV. 25)	Water and Water/Poison

Go over to the Pokémon Center in Zapapico right now.

The next Pokemon Center, which is northeast of here and near to Team Star's Poison Crew HQ, is where we must proceed. If you stand at the Pokémon Center in Zapacico and look northeast, you should be able to see the one we're going to. Move northeast and climb the hill to get an Ultra Ball. Go around the barrier and over the rocks to reach the Pokémon Center more quickly. There should be a second item, an antidote, and a different trainer to fight.

Trainer Name	Pokemon (w/ LV.)	Type
Veronica the Student	Greedent (LV. 25) / Gumshoos (LV. 25)	Normal and Normal

Go to the Pokémon Center if you need to unwind. Before heading to the Team Star Poison Crew HQ, continue east along the trail from Veronica the Student to find another trainer to complete the required amount of matches for a prize.

Trainer Name	Pokemon (w/ LV.)	Type
Judith the Student	Finizen (LV. 24)	Water

Don't forget to take the Revive from the top of the trash behind Veronica once you've defeated her. Go to the Pokémon Center if you need to unwind. From here, you can go straight to the Team Star Poison Crew headquarters in Tagtree Thicket. West of the Pokemon Center are the flags with the star logo in purple, green, and blue. An X Accuracy is available from the tree adjacent to the entrance. When you arrive at the base's gates and are getting close to Tagtree Thicket, the sequence will begin. You won't have to deal with a Team Star Grunt this time. Instead, you'll have to battle Pokemon Trainer Youssef.

Trainer Name	Pokemon (w/ LV.)	Type
Pokemon Trainer Youssef	Gulpin (LV. 30) / Shroodle (LV. 31)	Poison and Poison/Normal

Youssef's Pokemon are both susceptible to Ground and Psychic-type moves, so focus on using those here.

How Star Barrage Works

You have ten minutes to annihilate as many as thirty Pokemon during a Star Barrage. In order to choose three Pokemon that are weak to the Star Crew's type, you should concentrate on Psychic and Ground-type Pokemon for this one. To send your three Pokemon out and begin the battle at the same time as the timer, press R. In particular, we advise doing this frequently if you lose any Pokemon. To help them recover, Clive will be there. Utilize any of the scattered vending machines to refill your Pokemon. If you fail all three, the challenge must be restarted. When this happens, you'll also receive advice on the Pokemon varieties you should be using.

Challenge Atticus, Team Star's Poison Crew Boss

Lv.	Pokemon
Lv. 32	Skuntank
Lv. 33	Revraroom
Lv. 32	Muk
Lv. 32	Revaroom - Navi Starmobile

Against Atticus' Pokemon, you must without a doubt employ Ground-type attacks. However, you might also choose Fire-type Pokemon that are quite strong against Revaroom.

Rewards for Beating Atticus

You'll see a flashback involving everyone from Team Star once again once you've defeated Atticus. In addition to their Star Badge, Atticus will also give you TM102 Gunk Shot. Cassiopeia will get in touch with you when the battle is complete and give you 7,000 LP in addition to the materials you need to create the new TMs that will be made available once the base is finished.

Medali Gym (Normal)
How to Find Medali Gym (Normal)

You should return to Zapapico and leave from the west once you've vanquished Team Star Poison Crew - Atticus. This will start to bring you down the Dalizapa Passage in the direction of Glaseado Mountain and Medali. As you start along this path, you might come across your first Pokemon trainer on the right.

Trainer Name	Pokemon (w/ LV.)
Sara the Musician	Toxtricity (LV. 35)

Continue along the road while heading northwest. Grab the Hyper Potion from the area near the boulder just before the road starts to bend to the right. Stay on the path up until the signs that indicate a split in the road. Take the right-hand branching road that leads to Medali. Take the three extra super potions from the rocks when you turn right, and then enter the cave. On the way there, stop and talk to the trainer.

Trainer Name	Pokemon (w/ LV.)
Teo the Student	Tauros (LV. 36)

The Max Ether may be found on the left just before the cave entrance. Take the Rare Bone from the cave when you start to follow the route.Turn left to pick up the Hyper Potion after traveling west, and then turn right to confront the trainer.

Trainer Name	Pokemon (w/ LV.)
Mihai the Student	Hariyama (LV. 38)

Now exit the hallway and, if required, take a break in the Pokémon Center.From here, head west towards Medali's general direction. Once you have the Meditite Sweat, go outdoors to find the last foe you need to take care of in order to return to the Pokemon Center and collect your reward.

How to Prepare for Medali Gym (Normal)

Before you take on this Normal-type Gym, you should be level 36 or higher and have a team of Pokemon that are suitable for the assignment. When battling a gym that uses Normal-type Pokemon, we'd suggest using Fighting-type moves.

Recommend Level	Recommended Pokemon	Rewards Upon Completion
36	Fighting	TM025 Facade

How to Pass the Gym Test

As soon as you enter the Medali Gym, Nemona will greet you. Although she will want to fight you, as you might anticipate, she also wants to develop her team, so she will give you temporary control of the Normal-type Gym. The front desk clerk will inform you that you must order a specific item from a concealed menu in order to pass the fitness test. To finish this, you must go to the Treasure Eatery. You just need to make the appropriate orders in order to pass. So what is the process?

How to Order the Correct Secret Item Menu at Medali Gym

You'll be made aware that there are three other people working on the same problem concurrently, and that each of them has been given a different suggestion to help them in their search for the hidden dish. In order to get the hints from the others, you must complete each job. The loser then has to give the winner the solution. After receiving your hint, you ought to leave. Pay a visit to the Treasure Restaurant, which is situated west of the gym. You can get your first hint here before you face the Pokemon Trainers. The suggestion to speak with a regular is made. Once inside, swivel to the back. If the meal needs a squeeze of lemon, you can ask the office worker in a suit who is seated at the counter, and he will tell you. You should immediately leave the restaurant since you need to explore Medali to find the trainers' tips.

Where to Find Secret Item Menu Clue: 1

To find the first trainer, leave the Treasure Restaurant and move southwest down the street. You may find Santiago the Student near the end of the road, across from a few benches.

Trainer Name	Pokemon (w/ LV.)
Santiago the Student	Dunsparce (Lv. 34)

When you defeat Santiago, he will reveal the solution: the Pokemon with the blue bird.

How to Find the Blue Bird Pokemon

A man sporting a blue bird Pokemon on his head may be found not far from the location where you fought Santiago. It is back in the direction of the restaurant on the same street. "Meedyum" serves as your cue.

Where to Find Secret Item Menu Clue: 2

From Santiago, proceed on the street in the northwest. As you get closer to the street's end, the Pokemon Center is on the left. Turn right (northeast) after reaching the stairs. A student may be contemplating the dish that is hidden just next to the tree.

Trainer Name	Pokemon (w/ LV.)
Gisela the Student	Ursaring (Lv. 34)

Once you've fought Gisela, she will reveal the hint, which is a shadowy region encircled by steps. Just have a conversation with her to learn more.

How to Find the Dark Spot Surrounded by Stairs

Gisel (whom you would have passed en route) will be waiting for you as you descend the stairs. Climb to the gate above the dark entrance and enter it. There will be some illegible lettering that says, "Fire Blast."

Where to Find Secret Item Menu Clue: 3

Turn southeast and stop as you get closer to the sandwich shop. To the east of here is another kid who needs a hint from you.

Trainer Name	Pokemon (w/ LV.)
Adara the Student	Gumshoos (Lv. 34) / Greedent (LV. 34)

The tip is to seek for anything that stands out among the other goods at one of the ice cream stands, which you'll learn after fighting Adara and speaking with her.

How to Find the Odd Ice Cream Stand

Not far from Adara, there is an ice cream stand. If you speak to the person manning the stand and look at the menu, you'll see that grilled rice balls are listed.

Secret Menu Item Answers

Now that you have acquired all the information, you have all the cues you require to disclose the restaurant's hidden menu item. When you return to the Treasure Eatery, speak with the waiter you see as you go in. As soon as an order is placed:

- **Grilled Rice Balls**
- **Medium Serving**
- **Extra crispy, Fire Blast style**
- **Lemon**

By placing the proper order, you can challenge the Gym Leader and turn the restaurant into the Medali Gym.

Challenge the Medali Gym Leader Larry

Larry has Normal-type Pokemon, therefore you'll need Fighting-type Pokemon or Fighting-type techniques if you wish to attack effectively.

Lv.	Pokemon
Lv. 35	Komala
Lv. 35	Dudunsparce
Lv. 36	Staraptor

Medali Gym Rewards

Your reward for defeating Gym Leader Larry is TM025 Facade.

Montenevera Gym (Ghost)

How to Prepare for Montenevera Gym (Ghost)

Recommend Level	Recommended Pokemon	Rewards Upon Completion
42	Ghost and Dark-type	TM114 Shadow Ball

How to Find the Montenevera Gym (Ghost)

Leave Medali Gym (Normal) using the path that is closest to the north (Area Three) in order to enter West Province. Walk on until you reach something near to a rock on the right. Go in the same direction after picking up the Ultra Ball.On the right, a little higher up, close to another rock, there might be a Burn Heal. You should start to see a waterfall and the path up the mountain. When you reach the trainer on the left, continue along the path.

Trainer Name	Pokemon (w/ LV.)	Type
Alfonso the Courier	Altaria (LV. 35) / Gogoat (LV. 35) / Drednaw (LV. 35)	Flying/Dragon and Grass and Water

To get the Max Potion after defeating Alfonso, move east (against him). The Revive may then be found close to the boulder (on the right) by continuing down the route. Stay on the trail and cross the bridge.Another trainer can be located a short distance up the trail if you keep going in the direction to the right.

Trainer Name	Pokemon (w/ LV.)	Type
Hiker Estela	Whiscash (LV. 31)	Water/Ground

By the tree on the left, directly behind Estela, you might discover a Hyper Potion. Turn right to find another trainer along the trail and to the north.

Trainer Name	Pokemon (w/ LV.)	Type
Backpacker Nil	Leafeon (LV. 38) / Farigiraf (LV. 38)	Grass and Normal/Psychic

The route you're traveling on will split in half when you fight Backpacker Nil. At this point, turn right to continue climbing Glaseado Mountain. Before you reach the mountain, there is another trainer here to battle on the left.

Trainer Name	Pokemon (w/ LV.)	Type
Vidal the Student	Toxicroak (LV. 37) / Clawitzer (LV. 37)	Poison/Fighting and Water

Once Vidal has been defeated and you have reached Glaseado Mountain, you can pick up the X. attack at the trail's beginning. Continue down the path until there is only snow left and no more grass. You can engage in one more trainer conflict here before unwinding in the Pokémon Center.

Trainer Name	Pokemon (w/ LV.)	Type
Roberto the Scientist	Jolteon (LV. 36)	Electric

Pull out onto the road that curves slightly to the northwest once you've past Roberto to head to the Pokémon Center. Now head northeast and move in the trainer's and item's direction. Pick up the Ice Heal and take on the trainer.

Trainer Name	Pokemon (w/ LV.)	Type
Xabier the Courier	Staraptor (LV. 36)	Normal/Flying

Go east from Xabier and grab the Rare Bone from the marker. After that, turn eastward and travel for the water to face another trainer.

rainer Name	Pokemon (w/ LV.)	Type
Valeria the Student	Tauros (Actually a Zoroark) (LV. 36) / Mismagius (LV.36) / Tauros (LV. 36)	Dark and Ghost and Fighting

You should now turn northeast and climb Glaseado Mountain farther.You will come to a trail that leads up the mountain to the east. On the left, a Max Ether may be obtained, while on the right, a trainer can be fought.

Trainer Name	Pokemon (w/ LV.)	Type
Hiker Manuela	Camerupt (LV. 41) / Dedenne (LV. 41) / Veluza (LV. 42)	Fire/Ground and Electric/Fairy and Water/Psychic

As you proceed east up the mountain, take the Max Potion by the tree on the right. You climb the right-hand path, collecting the Timer Ball along the way. You will now be heading west as you ascend the mountain. By the tree, you can get an Ether. Turn south and take on one more trainer before you reach Montenevera.

Trainer Name	Pokemon (w/ LV.)	Type
Eduardo the Student	Polteageist (LV. 36) / Dudunsparce (LV. 36)	Ghost and Normal

The gym located to the east once you've reached Montenevera. When you walk in, Professor Jacq will be there to welcome you. He will give you a Lucky Egg before he departs.Speak to the receptionist at this gym to learn what the test will include.

How to Pas the Gym Test - Opening Act

Speak with MC Sledge outside on the stage. He'll tell you that you'll need to fight some double battles, so you'll be using two Pokemon for this.You must win three straight matches in order to pass this gym challenge.

Trainer Name	Pokemon (w/ LV.)
Gym Trainer Tas	Shuppet (LV.40) and Greavard (LV. 40)
Gym Trainer Lani	Haunter (LV.40) and Misdreavius (LV.40)
Gym Trainer MC Sledge	Sableye (LV. 40) and Drifblim (LV. 40)

Employ Dark and Ghost-type attacks throughout each of these encounters. Your party should be led by your two strongest Pokemon so that you can use them whenever necessary. Once you've eliminated all three of the gym trainers, you can go up against Ryme, the Montenevera Gym's leader.Return to the gym and let a staff member know you passed after giving your Pokemon a break. She will ask you whether you're ready to take on RIP's MC and gym boss Ryme. When you are, just say "yes," and you will be put into battle.

Challenge the Montenevera Gym Leader Ryme

Similar to the Gym Test, you will be using a duo for this duel. When Ryme releases her final Pokemon, she will use her Tera Orb.

Lv.	Pokemon
Lv. 41	Banette
Lv. 41	Mimikyu
Lv. 41	Houndstone
Lv. 42	Toxtricity

Utilize your Tera Orb to match Ryme in the final round.

Montenevera Gym Rewards

If you defeat Ryme, she will give you a TM114 Shadow Ball, and with six Gym Badges, you may easily control and catch Pokemon up to LV. 50.Just when you're about to leave the gym, Hassel will reappear. He'll claim that as one of the Elite Four, he can't wait for you to get all of the gym badges because he's excited to compete against you in the future.

The Ending of Pokemon Scarlet and Violet Explained

As you descend to Area Zero, it becomes clear that something is amiss with the Professor. It sounds like the Professor is malfunctioning when you walk into Lab 4, which makes this very evident. It's disregarded as a communication technology issue, but once you enter the Area Zero Lab, it's clear that nothing is as it seems. It turns out that the explosion that killed the Professor and damaged Lab 4 was also responsible. They have been replaced by an AI professor (AI Sada or AI Turo depending on whether you have Pokemon Scarlet or Violet). The professor has been experimenting with a time machine and has released Paradox Pokemon into the Paldea region, it is revealed. We have already seen this contradiction Pokemon in the shape of the Quaking Earth Titan. This was Pokemon Scarlet's time-traveling Great Tusk and Pokemon Violet's futuristic Iron

Treads. The AI Professor will explain that you need the Scarlet/Violet Book to halt this experiment. They'll also tell you that once the book is elevated, they'll start fighting, and you'll have to win. Your adversaries will be the AI Professor and a group of Paradox Pokemon that will try to stop the Time Machine. The Paradise Protection Protocol is tenacious, much more so than the AI Professor thinks, and Koraidon/Miraidon will materialize to stop the shutdown. Currently, all Pokémon Balls are sealed, so you can only use your own Koraidon or Miraidon. Terastallizing Koraidon/Miraidon is the best tactic for overcoming this difficult battle while utilizing all of the Pokemon's abilities. The AI Professor will use the Time Machine to travel to either the distant past or the distant future after winning this conflict, which will lead to the destruction of the Paradise Protection Protocol.

Throughout their adventure inside Area Zero, Penny, Arven, and Nemona each come to certain realizations about their behavior and relationships with one another. While Penny makes the most of her hacking abilities, Arven deals with the loss of his parents.As they slowly travel back to their house in the distance, the credits will begin to roll.

After the Credits

Nemona, Penny, and Arven will be called to the director's office following the credits, and you will be waiting there with them. After a brief presentation, you will be given a Master Ball. When Nemona recommends another match, Geeta, the chairperson of the Pokemon League, will certainly appear. She seems to concur with Nemona that it would be a fantastic idea for staff and kids to compete against one another. Geeta will also inform you that she wants you to visit every gym so that you can mark each one again on your map and engage in further combat with it.

Things to Do First in Violet and Scarlet

Which Starter Pokemon to Choose

The first and frequently most important choice in every Pokémon game is which of the three starter Pokemon you choose to accompany you on your adventure. There is no right or wrong choice, but the benefits each will provide in the beginning are briefly described below:

Sprigatito

The Sprigatito starter is a Grass-type. The fastest-evolving new non-Legendary Pokemon also boasts a respectable Attack stat to make use of its rapid feet. It is the beginning Pokemon that moves the fastest. Unfortunately, it has the weakest beginning defense, and its type defense is as weak. When it matters, use this Pokemon to deal quick, powerful damage.

Fuecoco

The name Fuecoco refers to the Fire-type starter. Although it is the only Special Attacker and the slowest Starter, it has the highest HP and Defense. Although the types it is susceptible to are relatively common, its typing also turns into the beginners' most protected. Although Fuecoco is the overall most defensive option, it nevertheless has a high Special Attack stat.

Quaxly

The Quaxly starter is of the Water type. While it has similar defenses and speeds to Fuecoco and Sprigatito, it has a substantially greater attack stat. Although the typeface is ordinary compared to the others, it is quite offensive. Quaxly is the most evenly matched of the three, yet he excels as a great attacker.

Finish Up Business at School

Basically, finish the first objective, The First Day of School. Despite the temptation to deviate, which can really be rather gorgeous if you don't mind moving slowly, keeping on this path will get you to a Pokemon Center quickly, where you can meet up with friends and trade.You can complete this "prologue" in around an hour and a half if you simply focus on the storyline objectives. After finishing it, you'll be able to use Terastalizing and ride either Koraidon or Miraidon, giving you access to everything Scarlet and Violet actually have to offer. Quick tip: Use the kiosk next to the main desk to swiftly move between the school's numerous rooms (and classes).

Tutorials Are Actually Helpful, But Optional

Even seasoned trainers find the lectures in the optional courses your institution provides to be really helpful, so you might want to start there. As you progress, you'll get access to even more. You might even find some reading material about Paldea's history in the entrance area.

Go Shopping

The selection at Delibird Presentations expands as you progress, but a surprisingly large number of genuinely useful goods are available right away, including unique combat weapons and training tools that increase a Pokemon's stats more quickly.These held Power items temporarily hinder a Pokemon in battle, but in exchange, the Pokemon receives extra points that go toward one of its qualities permanently. Effort Values are the name for these.Just keep in mind that with Pokemon Scarlet and Violet, EV points are only awarded to Pokemon during genuine combat, not via Auto Battles. They won't automatically learn new moves in this way as they level up either!

Head for the Cliffs

You can now go wherever you want and complete the assignments on any of the three pathways. However, there is a "golden route" that is apparent in the walkthrough and is determined by level. Since there is no level scaling in Pokemon Scarlet and Violet, even if it could be difficult to find really high-level Pokemon, you won't be able to control them without enough gym badges. The Rock-type Stony Cliff Titan to the east is technically second on the optimal path, but defeating it grants you the ability to dash on your ride, which is arguably a much bigger reward than the gym that is only little easier to the west. Now you can travel to new places much more rapidly.

Take Time to Explore

Even though this one is quite obvious, look into it! Compete against those trainers, catch those Pokemon, and collect that goods. You can take part in the following, more significant actions while in Paldea:

- To activate a rapid trip point so you can return even if you stray from the main path, look for nearby Pokémon Centers or watchtowers.
- However, Tera Raids are very useful if you ever need to grind quickly or gain LP for shopping. Exploring will also help you level up more naturally.
- If you find yourself surrounded by strong Pokemon, open your menu to escape a fight, or keep a Pokemon

with Run Away in the front of your party so you can always... run away. You can conclude that you are most likely at a high-level area if a trainer's text box is dark and their Pokemon appear to be stronger than your lead Pokemon.

- You can always ask Nurse Joy for advice on what to do next, but she usually picks things based on convenience rather than difficulty, so she can give you advice that will make you miserable.

10 Pokemon Scarlet and Violet tips to help you be the very best

With the help of Pokemon Scarlet and Violet guidance, you may establish yourself in Paldea and learn the principles of battling, capturing, and solving the game's many puzzles. Because the game has lately added a lot more intricacies, it's imperative to have a few early advantages as you set out to find your prize. Those who require help adjusting to the new environment that lies ahead may benefit from our Pokemon Scarlet and Violet with tips and tricks.

Going North takes you to more dangerous areas

Although the idea is simple, the game becomes more difficult as you move further north in Paldea since Trainers and wild Pokemon both level up at the same time. Starting at the southernmost point of the island is the simplest option; as you ascend, the difficulty increases.

Use this to foresee what is ahead and

assess your level of readiness. By the time you get to the highest beaches and mountains, the wild Pokemon will be level 50 or higher, and the Trainers will be much tougher.

Go for the Titans first to unlock new powers

Once the Naranja Academy Treasure Hunt has begun, you can pick between the three tasks: The Way of Legends, where you combat Titan Pokemon; Victory Road, where you battle gym leaders; and Starfall Street, where you battle members of Team Star. With each enemy you eliminate, Koraidon or Miraidon gains a new skill, such as the capacity to glide, jump higher, traverse water, or even scale walls.

Hit wild Pokemon in the back for a free attack

Press B to covertly approach a wild Pokemon, then throw a Pokeball at its back to start a battle. You'll be able to stop the Pokemon in its tracks and gain a big edge because of the Pokemon's astonishment at the start of the battle. There's no reason not to, so try to catch wild Pokemon by surprise whenever you can.

Save Terastallizing for bosses and gym leaders

Terastallizing, a new power-up you can give your Pokemon, turns them into that type (which you can check in the description), and it intensifies all of their attacks to match that kind. For example, a Wooper's other types will be replaced by electric when you Terastallize it with an Electric Tera Type, and their electric attacks will deal significantly more damage. Terastallizing calls for prudence because new qualities are being added to your weaknesses and strengths. But when utilizing it, you must also be cautious. You can only Terastallize Pokemon with your Tera Orb once, and it loses its charge after that. This power usually needs to be restored at a Pokemon Center, therefore it's important to save it for tough battles and opponents.

You don't have to fight trainers - but you should anyway

You can only fight trainers when you want to because they no longer challenge you until you approach them and start a dialogue. The best way to get money is to consistently battle Pokemon while also gaining obvious EXP, something you won't get from battling wild Pokemon. If all you do is fight nature, you'll run out of money the next time you want to buy Pokeballs and potions.

You can fight gym leaders, Titans, and the Star Team in any order - but they won't match your level

Pokémon Scarlet and Violet allow you to fight gym leaders and other bosses in any order, but it does not mean they are all equally easy. Regardless of your level, challenging opponents are always stronger than simple ones. The difficulty level of adversaries never changes. By going to the map and looking at the emblem for that boss, you may learn more about what to expect, including hints and cues about how difficult they are and what order you should confront them.

Without badges, you can't use high-level Pokemon

You can travel quickly to high-level locations and even capture strong level 50 Pokemon, but unless you have the gym badges you obtain by fighting gym leaders, they won't listen to your commands. When you catch low-level Pokemon and level them up, badges become meaningless because they will then obey your commands. However, the high-level Pokemon you capture will ignore your commands if you lack enough badges. Additionally, the level of Pokemon you can collect and manage relies on how many badges you have rather than the hardest gym you've fought. Even if you defeat the highest level gym first, you can only manage Pokemon obtained below level 25 because you only have one badge. You'll have to fight the easier enemies in order to cure it.

Send out Pokemon for Let's Go and Autobattling whenever possible

By pressing R, a player can send out the first Pokemon in their party in Let's Go mode to follow them around, collect items, and Autobattle nearby wild Pokemon to earn experience points (EXP) for both the player and the party. It's a good habit to get into, though you should be cautious about who you use your higher level Pokemon against. Considering their level and type advantage, your Pokemon may get hurt even when they fight on their own in an autobattle. Make certain they can handle the challenge you are giving them.

Picnics and Sandwiches offer free temporary buffs

Sandwiches—even terrible ones like the one depicted above—are a significant source of power-ups in Pokemon Scarlet and Violet. Numerous sandwiches and dinners give your Pokemon a variety of bonuses and advantages, like XP, battle power, and even the chance to come across shiny Pokemon. If you have the necessary equipment, you may prepare sandwiches whenever you set up a picnic or buy them prepared from food vendors in cities. Keep a watch out for NPC picnickers while exploring because they'll give you free stuff.

Tera Raids offer unique Pokemon and lots of gifts

The Tera Raids, which are giant crystals where three other players—online or non-player characters—may join forces with you to fight a powerful Terastallized Pokemon of a rare Tera species, can be found while you explore. These raids are indicated by light beams. By defeating them, you can acquire that Pokemon, obtain Tera Shards (used to change the Tera Types of your own Pokemon after conquering Gym Leader Larry), and enjoy a song from the soundtrack. Engage in Tera Raids whenever you can to strengthen yourself.

Cheats and Secrets

Duplicating Shiny Pokemon Spawns

Even the highly rare shining Pokémon may be easily duplicated in Pokémon Scarlet and Violet thanks to a bug. This bug prevents you from finding a shiny Pokemon, which only appear 1 in 4000 times. But if one does, it might point you in the direction of more copies.The vulnerability was described in a video provided by YouTuber Austin John Plays, according to Nintendo Everything, and it allows players to duplicate any wild pocket monster in the game. The Pokemon that spawn nearby any of the following cities are currently most vulnerable to this exploit: Los Patos, Cortondo, Cascarrafa,

Porto Marinada, Medli, Monternevera, Zapapico, Levincia, and Artazan. To use this hack on a Pokémon near a town, simply capture the Pokémon you want to clone. Grab it and head right for the town. You must run or ride a bike to the town in order for it to work; quick travel is not an option.Enter the town once its name appears in the middle of the screen. When the name of the town shows, save your work before quitting the game entirely. Go return to where you caught the Pokemon you wanted to clone after starting the game. Clone of the Pokemon you previously caught has taken its place. You can return to the town after catching the clone, wait for the name, save your game, quit the game, resume play, and repeat the process.

Double Running Speed

After it was first revealed on Reddit, players discovered that you can sprint twice as quickly by connecting two controllers simultaneously and hitting both left joysticks at the same time. IGN's

Rebekah Valentine put the vulnerability to the test using two Joy-Con controllers connected to the Nintendo Switch and a wireless Pro Controller, showing that it works.But we've found that it has a few shortcomings. It only works when you're using a portable gaming device. Additionally, the speed only rises when traveling diagonally. Although there is a notable improvement in speed, sprinting in zigzags is largely required to make the most of it.Finally, This hack only works when your character is moving forward. It doesn't seem to trigger while on the Miraidon or Koraidon. Therefore, instead of travelling in this manner, it would be best for you to ride them once you have a mount. However, this hack may lead to some more exciting discoveries in the future.

Titan Pokemon

Titan Pokemon Explained

There are five Titan Pokémon in the area of Paldea. Some Pokémon have gotten boosts from eating different Herba Mystica varieties. Arven's Trail of Legends mission requires him to find and defeat each of these giants. For every Titan you defeat, Koraidon/Miraidon gains a unique ability enhancement. The recommended level you should reach before coming here, the Pokemon you should have on your team, and the abilities each Pokemon unlocks for Koraidon/Miraidon are all listed in the table below. Each Titan possesses a special combination of powers and limitations.

Klawf, the Stony Cliff Titan

Recommend Level	Recommended Pokemon	Ability Unlocked
15	Grass, Water, or Ground-type Pokemon.	Dash for Mount

Bombirdier, the Open Sky Titan

Recommend Level	Recommended Pokemon	Ability Unlocked
19	Rock, Fairy, or Electric-type Pokemon.	Swimming

Orthworm, the Lurking Steel Titan

Recommend Level	Recommended Pokemon	Ability Unlocked
28	Fire, Fighting, or Ground-type Pokemon.	High Jump

Tatsugiri, the False Dragon Titan

Recommend Level	Recommended Pokemon	Ability Unlocked
55	Grass or Electric-type (for the first part of the encounter). Dragon or Fairy-type Pokemon.	Climbing

How to Catch the Titan Pokemon

You should be aware that you won't be starting with a large Pokémon. When you defeat them and take away their Herba Mystica supply, the Pokemon will have returned to a resemblance of normal size. However, they will have the best numbers imaginable and the biggest size for their species. Additionally, each of them will have the "Titan Mark" and might be referred to as "___ the Former Titan."You can return the next day to the location where you fought any of the Titan Pokemon from the Trail of Legends adventure to see the now-shrunken Titan hanging out. If you bump into them or lob a Poke Ball at them, nothing happens. To start the fight, you must approach them and converse with them. Make careful to manually save your game before turning off auto-saving. You can continue the game in this way if you mistakenly force them to pass out or fail the catch.

How to Equip the Titan Mark

After catching a Titan Pokemon, you can use their mark or title when adding them to your party. There, select Check Summary. Navigate to the tab all the way to the right, then press A to reveal the mark. During Trainer battles and if you swap Pokemon in the middle of a battle, you will now proudly claim that a Pokemon was a "Former Titan."

How to Catch Klawf, the Stony Cliff Titan

Klwaf the Former Titan might be at the South Province (Area Three) Watchtower. The entrance to the Herba Mystica cave is visible. To the right of the cave's entrance, there is a small path that ascends the mountain. Continue along the road until you see the Former Titan blocking your path. Their grade will be sixteen.

How to Catch Bombirdier, the Open Sky Titan

Near the base of the mountain is where you first saw Bombirdier, the Former Titan. Northwest of it is the "West

Province (Area One) - Central" Pokemon Center. If you take the winding path up to the spot where the stones were falling, you will see The Former Titan hovering right where the passage opens out. They will be at level 20.

How to Catch Orthworm, the Lurking Steel Titan

In close proximity to Orthworm the Former Titan lies the East Province (Area Three) Guard Tower. You can find it if you rapidly move to the hole near the tower. They will be at level 29.

How to Catch Great Tusk/Iron Treads, the Quaking Earth Titan

The Big Tusk/Iron Treads can be found on the western outskirts of the Asado Desert. A massive stone ring encircles it. They will be at level 45. It's crucial to remember that this is the first and only Paradox Pokemon in the game that can be found outside of Area Zero.

How to Catch Tatsugiri, the False Dragon Titan

You're still standing where you first found Tatsugiri the Former Titan. close to the edge of the tiny island, on the eastern side of Casseroya Lake. 57 levels will be present.

Picnics

Picnics in Pokemon Scarlet and Violet are an opportunity to interact with your Pokémon. During this period, you can make sandwiches, bathe your Pokémon, get Pokemon Eggs, and talk to them. Your entire squad, together with your legendary Pokemon Koraidon or Miraidon, are welcome to come outside for a break. You can personalize a few aspects of your picnic, including the dinnerware and Pokemon balls you use.

Sandwiches

This time, you can make a sandwich for your Pokemon as special group food. Before you can begin eating, you must first choose your sandwich, fillings, and toppings. These must be balanced and stacked correctly in order for them to stay on the bread at all! If your meal is good enough, it might also give you advantages that will help you in battle and capture in addition to healing your Pokemon. Your Pokemon will spend their free time as they choose, and they'll probably look cute doing it. These moments can be captured with the new image features! It is possible to snap group photos and then edit them with fun filters. Additionally, you can use Nintendo Switch Online to take images of friends that you might invite to picnics, so this feature isn't just for your Pokémon.

Cleaning Your Pokemon

Pokemon Scarlet and Violet allow you to clean your Pokemon after a battle or if you take them into the overworld with you, similar to Pokemon Amie and Pokemon Refresh in more recent years. Restoring their HP and raising their level of devotion for you will occur when you clean them up.

Eggs

In Pokemon Scarlet and Pokemon Violet, getting Pokémon Eggs requires hosting a picnic.

Where to Get and Use Bottle Caps

Where to Buy Bottle Caps

Bottle Caps will become accessible at each Delibird Presents Shop once you have finished the Victory Road quest and defeated your sixth Gym. The price of a bottle cap is 20,000p. They can be bought with cash or LP. The stores have an infinite supply of them. You will always be able to buy them as long as you have the money.

Get Bottle Caps From Raids

Bottle Caps are a rare reward that may also be acquired by participating in 6-Star Tera Raid Battles. Even while they are still rare, 6-Star Raids greatly increase your chances of obtaining one or more Bottle Caps. Additionally, there is a greater chance that Special Event Raids with 5 stars or more will reward you with Bottle Caps.

Gold Bottle Caps

Rare and hard to get Gold Bottle Caps occasionally appear at the Porto Marinada sale. But bear in mind that LP is not accepted; the auction only accepts cash payments. To make the winning offer, you will also require a large sum of money. One gold bottle cap is roughly equivalent to six regular bottle caps. As a result, you should charge no less than 120,000p for each Golden Bottle Cap. To stay inside your spending limit, bear this in mind while putting your offer.

How to Use Bottle Caps - Hyper Training

In the cold village of Montenevera, which is a part of north Paldea, is where you'll find the Ghost-Type Gym. Your Pokémon will receive Hyper Training from another town resident. They may be observed in the neighborhood of the town's Pokemon center standing near to an Abomasnow. He only accepts Bottle Caps as payment and will Hyper Train any Pokémon that is level 50 or higher. Each stat you raise costs one Bottle Cap.

How Hyper Training Works

Hyper-training can raise a Pokemon's IVs (Individual Values). These effectively define the six main stats of a Pokemon: HP, Attack, Defense, Sp. Attack, Sp. Def, and Speed. You can spend one Bottle Cap for each stat you desire to Hyper Train. Because your Pokemon has reached its maximum potential in the stats with a small crown next to them, they cannot be Hyper Trained. If you complete the Victory Road quest and defeat the Elite Four, you'll receive the Judge function. You can use this to see the IV ranking of your Pokemon. "Best" designates the stat's highest potential value for that Pokemon. From best to worst, the following terms are listed: Best, Fabulous, Very Excellent, Very Good, Decent, and No Good.Through hypertraining, the stat is virtually raised to the "Best" level. It will, however, mark the Pokemon as "Hyper Trained" because this isn't its natural IV. Hyper Trained stats are not passed on through breeding like the

Pokemon's initial IVs.

Where to Get and How To Use Ability Capsule and Ability Patch

What do Ability Capsule and Ability Patch do in Pokemon Scarlet and Violet?

The majority of Pokemon have a second Ability that may be revealed via an ability capsule; however, an ability patch exposes a secret Ability. Give your Pokemon a capsule or patch to alter its ability. When you give a Pokemon a capsule or patch, the new or concealed Ability will completely replace its old Ability. A Pokemon can only use one Ability at time.

Where to get Ability Capsule

You must first complete the full main story of Scarlet and Violet, including the post-game tale. Ability Capsules can be purchased from Chansey Supply Stores for 100,000 dollars once the game is finished. Chansey Supply Stores can be found at Mesagoza, Cascarrafa, Levincia, and Montenevera.Additionally, a capsule · may drop in Tera Raid Battles with 5 Stars (or higher).

Where to get Ability Patch

In 6 Stars Tera Raid Battles, an Ability Patch has a chance to drop. Be prepared to slog through multiple Tera Raid Battles because patches are an extremely uncommon drop.

Evolution Items - How to Evolve Every Pokemon

How to Evolve Gimmighoul

When Gimmighoul levels up after acquiring 999 Gimmighoul Coins, it transforms into Gholdengo.

Gimmighoul **Gholdengo**

**Level up
w/999
Gimmighoul
Coins**

How to Evolve Finizen

While in Union Circle, Finizen transforms into Palafin at level 38. (in co-op mode.)

Finizen   →   Palafin

                      Lv. 38, Union Circle

How to Evolve Charcadet

Charcadet becomes into Armarouge when wearing Auspicious Armor. Charcadet transforms into Ceruledge after you give it Malicious Armor.

Charcadet   →   Armarouge

                      Auspicious Armor

Charcadet   →   Ceruledge

                      Malicious Armor

How to Evolve Pawmo

When Pawmi reaches Level 18, Pawmo is born. In order for Pawmo to evolve into Pawmot, you must first let the Pokemon out of its Poke Ball and allow it to walk freely in Let's Go mode. This brand-new, special method is used to do this. The easiest, most efficient way to evolve them is to simply release them with ZR and let them run in a circle for two minutes without stopping. Seriously. We advise traveling to an open place in a city to prevent having to worry about wild Pokemon. Before the two minutes are up, if they go back to their Poke Ball, they might not grow. Level up candies by engaging in combat and using rare, EXP, or both types of candies.

Pawmi	→	Pawmo	→	Pawmot
Lv. 18		Walking w/o Poke Ball for 2 minutes		

How to Evolve Bramblin

Bramblin turns into Brambleghast after two minutes of continuous walking with it.

Bramblin	→	Brambleghast
	Continuous walking with it for 2 minutes	

How to Evolve Dunsparce

Dunsparce becomes Dudunsparce when it levels up and is aware of the maneuver. Excessive Drill

Dunsparce	→	Dudunsparce
	Level up knowing Hyper Drill	

How to Evolve Girafarig

Girafarig becomes Farigiraf as he gains experience and masters Twin Beam.

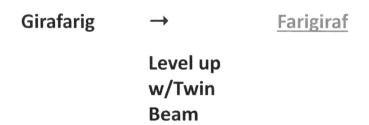

Girafarig	→	Farigiraf
	Level up w/Twin Beam	

How to Evolve Bisharp

Pawniard changes into Bisharp at Level 52. Bisharp transforms into Kingambit by holding Leader's Crest and taking out three additional Bisharp that are surrounding it.

How to Evolve Primeape

Mankey transforms into Primeape at level 28. After 20 times of utilizing Rage Fist, Primeape level ups and changes into Annihilape. Primeape learns Raging Fist at level 35.

Mankey	→	Primeape	→	Annihilape
Lv. 28		Leveling up after using Rage Fist 20 times		

How to Evolve Capsakid
Giving a Fire Stone to Capsakid allows it to change into Scovillain.

How to Evolve Tadbulb
Tadbulb changes into Bellibolt when a Thunder Stone is used.

How to Evolve Cetoddle
Cetoddle turns into Cetitan when given an Ice Stone.

How to Evolve Scyther
Scizor is created when Scyther is exchanged while covered in a Metal Coat.

How to Evolve Slowpoke
By trading while carrying a King's Rock, Slowbro can evolve into Slowking at Level 37, and Slowking can evolve into Slowbro.

How to Evolve Sneasel

Sneasel turns into Weavile if a Razor Claw is left in its possession at night.

How to Evolve Pikachu

When two people are very close, Pichu changes into Pikachu. Pikachu changes into Raichu thanks to the Thunder Stone.

How to Evolve Charcadet into Armarouge and Ceruledge

How to Get Charcadet Early and Evolve It
Watch the video above or read on for a brief summary of how to swiftly acquire Charcadet in the early game and how to evolve it in both Scarlet and Violet.You should eat a Pickle Sandwich (only pickles and olive oil) to get the Fire Encounter food power.Next (Area Three), the Pokémon Center in South Province. Charcadet should be straightforward to go there with the meal power!

How to Evolve Charcadet Into Armarouge

In Pokemon Scarlett, Charcadet may turn into Armarouge by using a special item. Only a man in Zapapico sells the Auspicious Armor, and it only works with Pokemon Scarlet. He will be loitering in the town's center, looking for anyone who might be interested in doing business. He will give you the Auspicious Armor in exchange for ten Bronzor fragments. among Pokemon Scarlet, Steel- and Psychic-type Bronzor are frequently discovered among ruins, and they can be defeated or captured to get these resources.

How to Evolve Charcadet Into Ceruledge

In Pokemon Violet, Charcadet can evolve into Ceruledge by using a special item. The unique Malicious Armor may only be given to Pokémon Violet by a woman in Zapapico. She will be loitering around the town's center, looking for anyone who might be interested in a deal. She will give you the Malicious Armor if you give her 10 Sinistea Chips. These goods can be obtained by capturing or eliminating Sinistea, a Black Tea Pokemon of the Ghost type.

How to Find the Armor for Charcadet

Charcadet's Adventures is a book about Charcadet and its development, located on the third floor of the Entrance Hall's right side.

Auspicious Armor: Where to Find Bronzor - Bronzor Fragments

To maximize the amount of materials you might get during bouts with Bronzor, we advise ingesting a meal that contains the enhancement "Item Drop Power: Psychic".The advantage of Bronzor is that, especially at night, they are regularly seen in and around many of Paldea's ruins. Auto battles, which are completed far more quickly than regular contests, are the quickest way to defeat them. To obtain the Auspicious Armor, travel to Zapapica and present your ten Bronzor Pieces to the mysterious man there. They must be a part of your party for

Charcadet to develop The Auspicious You may locate armor on the tab with the candy-icon emblem in your bag. Choose it, then select Charcadet if you want them to start growing immediately away. The signature move of Armarouge is the Fire-type special attack known as Armor Cannon. One of Armarouge's most powerful techniques, albeit it lowers Armarouge's characteristics for Defense and Sp. Defense in exchange for its strength.

Malicious Armor: Where to Find Sinistea - Sinistea Chips

Sinistea is most frequently seen in the area surrounding Alfornada. This town, which is southwest of the Paldea region, is where the Psychic-type Gym is situated. The Sinistea and other Pokemon there are leveling in the mid-30s to low-40s. You shouldn't go there at the start of the game because of this. Once you have a strong crew and have attained a sufficient level, travel to Alfornada. Sinistea roam the pastures on the town's southern outskirts. But the best place to find them in vast numbers is the ruins atop the mountain just outside the town's eastern border. They are accessible every hour of the day, regardless of the weather. You can acquire Sinistea Chips by defeating Sinistea in matches. For beating Sinistea, you will also receive at least one Sinistea Chip and maybe as many as two. Your best course of action is to engage in auto fights because you can eliminate more Sinistea that way than if you try to capture or engage each one individually. Travel to Zapapica and give the mysterious woman there 10 Sinistea Chips to receive the Malicious Armor. They must be a part of your party for Charcadet to develop. The tab with the candy-icon icon in your purse contains the harmful armor. Choose it, then select Charcadet if you want them to start growing immediately away. Pokemon Violet's Charcadet development potential is unrestricted because to the Malicious Armor's multiple acquisition possibilities.

Each time you offer her 10 Sinistea Chips, she will gift you a fresh set of nasty armor. After evolving, Charcadet is capable of learning the Ghost-Type move Shadow Claw. Ceruledge's signature move, Bitter Blade, can be learned at Level 48. It is an accurate physical attack of the fire type with a basic power of 90. Additionally, using it can replenish Ceruledge's HP by up to half the damage the victim has taken.

How to Evolve Bisharp into Kingambit

Bisharp Location for Catching

A Bisharp is need first. A Pawniard can become a Bisharp at level 52, or you can hunt one down in the Bamboo Groves of North Province (Area 2).But since you'll also need a brand-new held item called the Leader's Crest, you'll want to keep a look out for a specific Bisharp.

Get a Leader's Crest

This item will only be owned by a select few Bisharp, most notably Bisharp who are in charge of a group of Pawniard, as implied by the item's description. You're looking for a Pawniard cluster with a Bisharp in the center.To get the item, you can either use Thief on the Bisharp to catch it or use Leader's Crest to capture it. The item can be obtained without further effort—Compound Eyes are not necessary! because every Bisharp we found with Pawniard surrounding it has a Leader's Crest. When you obtain a Leader's Crest, give it to your Bisharp to hold.

Defeat Three Specific Bisharp with Your Bisharp

Now that you have a Bisharp in possession of a Leader's Crest, you must test its strength by putting it to the test against three other Bisharp who also hold the item. Similar to how you could tell who was a good opponent when you received a Leader's Crest, you can do so now. Attack a trio of Bisharp that are under Pawniard siege. It is suggested that you teach your Bisharp a fighting-style move. Bisharp can learn the Fighting-type move Low Kick with the aid of a TM. This move deals other Bisharp four times as much damage as it does to you, so you should be able to one-shot them!

Level Bisharp Up

After facing three of them, the right Bisharp can now become a Kingambit by simply leveling up once. Bisharp can level up by engaging in combat with other Pokemon, using Rare Candy, EXP Candy, or both.

How to Evolve Pawmo, Bramblin, and Rellor - New Evolution Method

How to Evolve Pokemon With the Let's Go! Feature

These Pokémon will evolve after you've walked beside them for a while, regardless of whether you've let them out to combat in Let's Go mode with R or are simply strolling with them with ZR. However, it might be tough to keep them out and moving as this method looks to be dependant on the motions you make since they typically do not keep up with you when walking. Whichever you're developing, simply letting them run with

ZR and having them run in a circle without pausing for two minutes is the quickest and simplest way to evolve them. Seriously. We advise traveling to an open place in a city to prevent having to worry about wild Pokemon. Before the two minutes are up, if they go back to their Poke Ball, they might not grow. After that, level them up once by engaging in combat with them and/or using rare, EXP, or both types of candies. They won't grow if they level up via an Auto Fight.

Made in the USA
Monee, IL
09 September 2023

42433000R00072